Texas Bats

W9-ABZ-704

by Merlin D. Tuttle

Copyright 2003 by Bat Conservation International, Inc.
ISBN # 0-9638248-8-0

Requests for permission to reproduce material from this work should be sent to: Bat Conservation International, P.O. Box 162603, Austin, Texas 78716.

Acknowledgements

The author gratefully acknowledges invaluable assistance from the following individuals and agencies. Funding was made possible through the generous support of Travis and Betina Mathis, The Brown Foundation, the U.S. Fish and Wildlife Service, the Texas Parks and Wildlife Foundation, and the Houston Endowment.

Annika Keeley, in her capacity as Texas Bat Coordinator for the Texas Parks and Wildlife Department and Bat Conservation International, assembled much of the supporting information for this publication. Angela England prepared range maps, and she and Paul Robertson contributed extensive review. Robert Locke provided substantial editorial assistance, and Elysia Wright Davis designed the publication.

Contents

Introduction 4
Frequently Asked Questions .5
Anatomy of a Bat 14
Leaf-chinned Bats
 Peters's Ghost-faced Bat 16
Leaf-nosed Bats
 Mexican Long-tongued Bat 19
 Mexican Long-nosed Bat 20
Vesper Bats
 Pallid Bat 23
 Rafinesque's Big-eared Bat 24
 Townsend's Big-eared Bat 26
 Big Brown Bat 27
 Spotted Bat 28
 Silver-haired Bat 29
 Western Red Bat 30
 Eastern Red Bat 32
 Hoary Bat 34
 Southern Yellow Bat 35
 Northern Yellow Bat 36
 Seminole Bat 38
 Western Yellow Bat .39
 Southeastern Myotis .40
 California Myotis 42
 Western Small-footed Myotis 44
 Little Brown Myotis .46
 Northern Myotis 48
 Fringed Myotis 50
 Cave Myotis 52
 Long-legged Myotis .53
 Yuma Myotis 54
 Evening Bat 56
 Western Pipistrelle 57
 Eastern Pipistrelle 58
Free-tailed Bats
 Greater Bonneted Bat 60
 Pocketed Free-tailed Bat 61
 Big Free-tailed Bat .62
 Mexican Free-tailed Bat 64
Bat Watching in Texas 66
Books about Bats 69
Contact Information 71

Introduction

Within the rich and varied medley of Texas wildlife, few creatures are as fascinating and beneficial as the Lone Star State's 32 species of bats. No other group of Texas mammals is more important to the balance of nature, and none is more diverse. Red, silver-haired, and spotted bats are strikingly colorful. Ghost-faced bats look as exotic as any dinosaur. Mexican free-tailed bats sing like warblers. Greater bonneted bats have narrow wings for jet-like flight, while big-eared bats fly like helicopters on broad wings. Most Texas bats eat insects, often those that farmers find most damaging, and bats have enormous appetites: A single Texas colony of free-tailed bats consumes billions of insects every summer night. Other bat species are essential pollinators of desert plants.

Yet bats, active only at night, are seldom seen, often misunderstood, and usually feared. Many people still believe bats are blind, flying mice that carry diseases and become tangled in women's hair. In truth, bats are more closely related to people than to mice, they generally have excellent eyesight, and they are far too clever to entangle themselves in anyone's hair. Bats seldom transmit disease to people or pets; when left alone, they are among our safest neighbors. Their fearsome reputation is completely undeserved.

Worldwide, there are more than 1,100 kinds of bats — nearly a fourth of all mammal species. Bats are found everywhere except in the most extreme desert and polar regions, although most live in tropical forests, where they feed on fruit, nectar, pollen, and insects. A few tropical species feed on small fish, frogs, mice, and birds.

Despite their notoriety, vampire bats, which do indeed feed on blood, account for only three of the world's species and live only in Latin America. Texas bats feed exclusively on insects, except for pallid bats that also prey on scorpions and centipedes, and long-nosed and long-tongued bats that eat nectar and pollen.

Frequently Asked Questions

Where do bats live?

In Texas, bats roost in caves, rock crevices, tree cavities, and foliage, as well as in bridges, buildings, abandoned mines, and bat houses (designed specifically for them). Each species has its own unique requirements. Disturbing or destroying caves can threaten thousands to millions of bats at a time, especially Mexican free-tailed bats, long-nosed bats, and cave myotis. Loss of old-growth forests deprives species such as Rafinesque's big-eared bats and southeastern myotis of the large tree hollows they require. Just trimming dead palm fronds can destroy roosts needed by yellow bats.

© MERLIN D. TUTTLE, BCI \ 831-5503

The fur of this hibernating eastern pipistrelle is covered with water droplets, which condense from the cave environment and keep the bat from dehydrating.

Where do bats go in winter?

Because food becomes scarce during cold weather, most Texas bats either hibernate or migrate to warmer climates. Some, such as evening and yellow bats that live in mild coastal climates, conserve energy by temporarily entering a dormant state called "torpor" during brief periods of cold weather; they become active and start feeding again on warmer nights. When in torpor or hibernation, bats reduce their metabolism and conserve energy by allowing their body temperature to fall to that of their surroundings. In the northernmost United States, hibernating bats survive up to eight months at a time on stored fat reserves, their body temperatures often dipping to just above freezing. In the northern half of Texas, hibernation

An eastern red bat mother roosts with her three pups beneath dense vines.

requires finding shelter in caves or mines. While in the deep sleep of hibernation, bats are extremely vulnerable to human disturbance and are easily killed by vandals. In addition, being awakened early forces them to burn fat they'll need to avoid starvation before spring.

How do bats court and rear young?

Bats, like humans, are mammals that court and mate, give birth to helpless young, and nurse them with milk. Like birds, males often lure mates by singing. Most mothers bear only one baby each year, one of many characteristics that set them apart from rodents. Bats typically mate in fall or winter but do not become pregnant until spring. Pups reach nearly adult size and learn to fly in three to five weeks.

How long do bats live?

All bats are exceptionally long-lived for their size. Individual bats have been captured by researchers, banded and released, then recaptured up to 34 years later, although the average life span is significantly less.

Are bats really blind?

Bats are not blind and many have excellent vision. But most bats also have another very powerful navigation aid called echolocation. They can fly at high speeds and hunt in total darkness by sending out high-frequency sounds and listening for echoes. Even when relying on sound alone, bats can "see" everything but color and detect obstacles as fine as a human hair.

Are bats dangerous?

Here are the facts: During the past 50 years, only 40 U.S. residents are believed to have contracted rabies from bats. To put this in perspective, consider that in an average year, 900 Americans die in bicycle accidents, 150 in accidents caused by deer, 20 from dog attacks, and 18 in lawn mower accidents. By simply not handling bats, the chance of contracting any disease from them becomes extremely small.

Most mammals can contract rabies, but less than one-half of one percent of bats become infected and these rarely attack people, even when sick. In a lifetime of studying bats worldwide, I have not seen a single bat become aggressive, except to bite in self-defense when it is being handled. The vast majority of bat bites result from careless handling and are easily felt at the time. The odds of contracting rabies from an unnoticed bite are about on a par with

© Merlin D. Tuttle, BCI \ 803-1401

This big brown bat has just caught a beetle — one of its favorite prey — to the delight of farmers.

© Merlin D. Tuttle, BCI \ 835-4106

Bats are especially vulnerable to human disturbance because many species, like these Mexican free-trailed bats, roost in large, conspicuous colonies.

the likelihood of being killed by a meteorite. In all cases, animals that bite humans should be tested for rabies; and unless the tests prove negative, anyone bitten should be vaccinated as soon as possible as a precaution. Modern rabies vaccines are safe and effective if administered soon after a possible exposure.

Aerosol rabies transmission (contracting the disease through the air) was hypothesized as a possible source of two human rabies cases from Texas bat caves some 40 years ago. No other potential cases have been reported, however, although thousands of Texas cavers have been exploring bat caves in the subsequent decades. No one has ever been infected from contact with bat droppings, urine, or blood.

Almost any mammal can transmit rabies. To ensure your family's safety, be sure to vaccinate all dogs and cats, regardless of whether bats are in your neighborhood, and warn children never to handle any unfamiliar animals.

Media stories attempting to link bats to other frightening diseases, such as ebola or swine flu, are based on pure speculation, without a single documented case of actual transmission — and these diseases do not occur in Texas. The only other disease that can be contracted from a bat in Texas is histoplasmosis, which is caused by a widespread fungus that lives in soil enriched by animal droppings. In the United States, histoplasmosis is most often found in and near the Mississippi and Ohio River Valleys. It is extremely common and most U.S. residents have been infected without even knowing it, usually by breathing dust associated with bird droppings. Symptoms are normally mild or undetectable, although inhaling large quantities of spore-laden dust can cause serious illness. This is most likely to occur while cleaning chicken coops or working around other concentrated bird roosts, although some careless cavers also have become seriously ill after inhaling large quantities of dust while crawling through cave passages or digging for artifacts in bat caves. The fungus that causes histoplasmosis seldom survives in hot, dry attics where bats roost, but when cleaning such places, it is nonetheless wise to wear a respirator that can filter out small fungal spores (down to two microns in diameter).

Are bats beneficial?

Bats are essential predators of insects that fly at night, just as birds are with daytime insects. Bats consume vast quantities of moths, beetles, crickets, leafhoppers, mosquitoes, and other insects, including many pests that cost American farmers and foresters billions of dollars a year.

In Central Texas alone, an estimated 100 million Mexican free-tailed bats eat roughly 1,000 tons (two million pounds) of insects every summer night. In spring, when such costly crop pests as corn earworm and armyworm moths are migrating north from Mexico, these bats intercept them thousands of feet above ground, eliminating billions in a single night. Each female moth carries about 1,000 eggs, so if a bat catches just 20, that single bat will have kept 20,000 eggs from being laid on crops. A farmer would have to spray approximately two acres with pesticides to achieve the same results as that one bat.

Another Texas species, the big brown bat, specializes in beetles, including the spotted cucumber beetle, whose corn rootworm larvae cost American farmers roughly a billion dollars a year. A colony of 150 big brown bats can catch enough cucumber beetles each summer to prevent them from laying 33 million eggs. Other Texas bat species consume forest pests, such as the pine bark beetle, that threaten timber.

Of more immediate concern to the average Texan: Small pipistrelle and myotis bats are such efficient foragers that they can detect, catch, and eat two or more mosquito-sized insects in a single second, up to 1,000 or more in an hour. One Florida colony of southeastern myotis, a species that also lives in the East Texas wetlands, consumes an estimated 11 tons of mosquitoes annually. Imagine the economic plight of Texas farmers, the frustration of urban gardeners, and the misery of backyard barbecuers without bats!

Do bats need protection?

Bats are extraordinarily important around the world, yet they are among our most misunderstood, intensely persecuted, and endangered animals.

Grossly exaggerated warnings of possible rabies transmission by bats in Texas and fear of vampire bats in Mexico pose severe threats to our shared migratory species. In Mexico, millions of highly beneficial bats have been deliberately killed when caves in which they spend the winters were burned, dynamited, or poisoned; many more have been destroyed in Texas and elsewhere in the American Southwest by needlessly frightened people. In Arizona's Eagle Creek Cave, the population of Mexican free-tailed bats plummeted from more than 25 million in 1960 to barely 30,000 just six years later, and at New Mexico's famous Carlsbad Caverns, free-tailed bat numbers have fallen some 95 percent since the 1930s.

In 1995, Bat Conservation International and the Institute of Ecology at Mexico's National Autonomous University collaborated to create the Program for the Conservation of Migratory Bats. Through that partnership, leading scientists and conservationists are now educating local communities and establishing nature reserves to protect key caves on both sides of our border. The battle to overcome human ignorance and fear continues.

Bats are virtually defenseless, and large colonies like ours in Texas make easy targets. A single act of vandalism can kill millions. Bats are exceptionally vulnerable because they often live in large, conspicuous colonies and females typically produce only one pup per year.

Mexican free-tailed bats emerge from their summer home in a bat house.

How can I help?

- Avoid disturbing or harming bats. If bats have moved into the attic or another part of your home and you want to get rid of them, offer them a bat house as an alternate home before excluding them.

- Tell your friends, colleagues, and neighbors about the fascinating nature of bats and help dispel their fears.

- Give bat programs for youth groups, local garden clubs, Lions Clubs, Rotary Clubs, etc. For more information and educational materials, contact Bat Conservation International at 512-327-9721 or Texas Parks and Wildlife at 512-912-7011.

- Provide bat houses. Simple and inexpensive, bat houses provide safe havens for bats and pay off as the bats reduce lawn and garden pests. You'll also find that you enjoy learning about bats and sharing your knowledge with friends and neighbors.

- Protect diverse wildlife habitats on your property, including water, snags, native plants, and old-growth vegetation. For information and management recommendations, contact Texas Parks and Wildlife (512-912-7011) or Bat Conservation International (512-327-9721).

I have a bat in my house. What do I do?

Bats that fly into human living quarters are usually lost youngsters whose primary goal is to get back outside as quickly as possible. They often leave on their own if a window or door is left open to the outside while those leading to the rest of the house are closed. Bats are not aggressive, even if chased, but they may bite in self-defense if caught. As with any wild animal, bats should not be handled with bare hands.

If the visitor won't leave on its own — or you run out of patience — you can remove it yourself. Catch the bat in flight with a hand net (swung from behind) or, once the bat lands, cover it with a coffee can and slip a piece of cardboard under the opening to trap the bat inside. Then simply release it outside. You may also catch a bat by hand if you use leather work gloves to avoid being bitten. Handle the bat gently.

Baby bats occasionally fall out of tree roosts. If you encounter young red bats on the ground, you can pick them up — while wearing leather work gloves — and hang them on a nearby tree, away from curious pets and children. Frequently, the mother will return for her wayward pup the following evening. If not, contact a local wildlife rehabilitator.

How can I get nuisance bats out of attics or wall spaces?

Bats can be excluded from human living quarters by covering chimneys and vents with screens of half-inch hardware cloth, by installing draft guards beneath doors, and by sealing any other possible access routes, especially around screen doors, windows, and plumbing. Bats can enter through holes as small as three-quarters of an inch in diameter or gaps measuring as little as three-eighths by seven-eighths of an inch. They do not chew insulation or make new holes. Their entries can be plugged with silicone caulk, steel wool, or, temporarily, with tape. If a bat colony must be evicted from a wall or attic, watch the bats as they emerge at dusk to feed. This will help you locate entry holes, which can sometimes be identified by stains around holes or crevices or by droppings beneath.

After the entrances are located, the bats can be excluded. Don't try that, however, when flightless pups may be present (usually May through August). Besides the needless cruelty of starving babies too young to fly away, the bodies of dead pups can create a serious odor problem.

Many Texas bats leave the area during winter, which offers an ideal time to bat-proof your home. For bats that remain year-round, or if you can't wait for winter, you can install a relatively simple one-way exclusion valve that allows bats to leave the house but not to return. During the daytime, when the bats are roosting, staple or tape a strip of plastic sheeting or lightweight polypropylene netting (with one-sixth-inch mesh) over each entry point. The strip should hang an inch or so in front of the opening and extend about a foot on each side and two feet below it. Seal the top and sides with tape or staples, leaving space only at the bottom, which should hang loosely so bats can exit as they emerge in the evening. Leave the material in place for two or three days to ensure that all the bats have left before permanently sealing the holes. For additional details, consult the Bat Conservation International Web site at www.batcon.org.

How can I attract bats to my yard?

With traditional roosts in trees and caves still being destroyed, many of North America's bats are forced to seek shelter in human-made structures. You can help bats by installing a bat house in your yard or by working with local parks and nature centers to make sure bats are included in their wildlife plans. To learn more about how to build and mount bat houses, visit Bat Conservation International's Web site at www.batcon.org. You can also purchase *The Bat House Builder's Handbook* or the *Building Homes for Bats* video or join the North American Bat House Research Project through the BCI catalog. Bat houses may also be purchased. Call 1-800-538-BATS or 512-327-9721 or order online at www.batcon.org.

What makes a bat house successful?

It pays to build or buy a quality bat house and to carefully caulk and paint it. Three coats of exterior paint will greatly increase the success of even the best houses. Bats don't like leaks or drafts any more than we do. Each winter, you should check for wasp nests that may require removal and repair any cracks or other problems that could cause leaks.

Bats like their houses located on the sides of wooden or stone buildings or on poles where they are relatively safe from predators and where they receive at least six hours of direct sun each day. That usually means bat houses should be at least 12 to 15 feet above ground and not closer than 20 feet to the nearest trees, which can obstruct the sun or provide perches for owls that hunt bats. Locations near streams, rivers, or lakes are preferred because of the aquatic insects they harbor.

Careful landlords are now achieving success rates of about 55 percent with single-chamber houses and 85 percent with multi-chambered houses. All bat houses do better when placed in groups of at least two or three, and even single-chambered houses are 72 percent successful when mounted on the sunny side of buildings, which improves solar heating. The most successful nursery houses are often mounted in back-to-back pairs on poles in full sun.

Great columns of Mexican free-tailed bats spread over the Central Texas countryside each summer evening from their roosts in Frio Cave.

ANATOMY OF A BAT

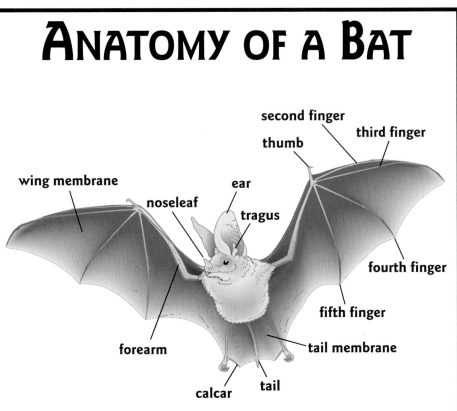

ILLUSTRATION BY DAVID CHAPMAN

second finger

third finger

thumb

wing membrane

ear

noseleaf

tragus

fourth finger

fifth finger

forearm

tail membrane

calcar

tail

Glossary

Calcar: A long, bony spur on the bat's ankle that helps support the tail membrane.

Forearm, fingers, and thumb: Bats' forelimbs include most of the same components as those of other mammals, but the hands and fingers are elongated to support and manipulate the wings.

Noseleaf: A cartilaginous flap of skin above the nostrils of some bats. Among American species with this feature, it usually is triangular and rises vertically from the tip of the nose.

Tail membrane: Also called the interfemoral membrane, this spans the area between a bat's legs and tail.

Tragus: A cartilaginous flap of skin at the base of the external ear. It often rises vertically like a small sword.

Wing membrane: A thin double layer of skin that forms the bat's flying surface.

Leaf-chinned Bats
FAMILY MORMOOPIDAE

Peters's Ghost-faced Bat (*Mormoops megalophylla*) 16

Peters's Ghost-faced Bat (*Mormoops megalophylla*)

Peter's Ghost-faced Bat
Mormoops megalophylla

ETYMOLOGY

Greek: *Mormoops* (monster bat);
Greek: *megalophylla* (large leaves).

APPEARANCE

Ghost-faced bats get their name from their rather bizarre appearance. They have conspicuous flaps of skin on the chin. Large, round ears join across the forehead, and their eyes appear to be located in their ears. Fur is reddish to dark brown. Forearm: 2.0 to 2.3 inches (51 to 59 mm). Wingspan: approximately 14.6 inches (370 mm).

MATING AND REARING YOUNG

Mating occurs in fall; one pup is born in late May to early June.

HABITAT AND FOOD

Peters's ghost-faced bats live in semiarid and desert areas, usually at elevations below 9,000 feet. Prey include large, soft-bodied moths, though this bat's diet is poorly documented.

ROOSTING BEHAVIOR

They most often roost in caves, rock crevices, and abandoned mines, although they occasionally move into old buildings. Colonies in Latin America may contain up to 500,000 individuals. Roosting sites are often shared with cave myotis and Mexican free-tailed bats. Nursing mothers roost in the warmest areas of occupied caves, while males and non-reproducing females roost separately from the nursing mothers. Both sexes remain active year-round, except during extreme weather, and make only relatively local movements among roosts.

HUMAN ENCOUNTERS

Peters's ghost-faced bats are rarely encountered by people. Cavers occasionally find colonies roosting in caves and should avoid disturbing them.

Leaf-nosed Bats
FAMILY PHYLLOSTOMIDAE

Mexican Long-tongued Bat (*Choeronycteris mexicana*) 19

Mexican Long-nosed Bat (*Leptonycteris nivalis*) 20

Mexican Long-tongued Bat
Choeronycteris mexicana

ETYMOLOGY

Greek: *Choeronycteris* (nocturnal pig);
Latin: *mexicana* (belonging to Mexico).

APPEARANCE

Mexican long-tongued bats have long, slender noses with a leaf-like projection at the tip. Tails are short but clearly visible. Fur is sooty gray to brownish. Forearm: 2.0 to 2.3 inches (51 to 59 mm). Wingspan: 13 to 14.2 inches (330 to 360 mm).

MATING AND REARING YOUNG

Mating probably occurs in spring. Mothers give birth to a single pup in late June to early July. Unlike many other bat babies, Mexican long-tongued bats are already furred and well developed at birth. Juveniles learn to fly within two to three weeks.

HABITAT AND FOOD

Mexican long-tongued bats occupy a variety of habitats, including thorn scrub, palo verde/saguaro desert, semidesert grassland, oak woodland, and tropical deciduous forests. They are believed to migrate seasonally, following the flowering and fruiting cycles of the plants on which they feed. Primary foods are nectar and pollen of night-blooming plants, especially agaves, and the nectar, pollen, and fruit of columnar cacti.

ROOSTING BEHAVIOR

They most often roost in caves, mines, rock crevices, and abandoned buildings. Colonies usually consist of up to 15 individuals, but some may include 40 to 50 bats. Colonies remain active year-round, except during extreme weather. Those that visit Texas in summer likely migrate to warmer climates in Mexico for winter.

HUMAN ENCOUNTERS

Mexican long-tongued bats live in places where they seldom encounter humans, although they sometimes visit hummingbird feeders.

Mexican Long-nosed Bat (*Leptonycteris nivalis*)

Mexican Long-nosed Bat
Leptonycteris nivalis

ETYMOLOGY

Greek: *Leptonycteris* (slender and nocturnal);
Latin: *nivalis* (snowy).

APPEARANCE

Mexican long-nosed bats have long muzzles with a noseleaf at the tip. Fur is sooty brown. Unlike Mexican long-tongued bats, the tails of Mexican long-nosed bats are too short to be seen; and tail membranes barely exist as a fringe. Forearm: 2.2 to 2.4 inches (55 to 60 mm). Wingspan: approximately 16.1 inches (410 mm).

MATING AND REARING YOUNG

One pup is born between April and June. Young are typically born in Mexico, before the bats' northward migration into the Big Bend area.

HABITAT AND FOOD

Mexican long-nosed bats synchronize their arrival in Texas with the summer blooming cycle of agave plants, on which they rely for nectar and pollen. In Mexico, they also eat the nectar, pollen, and fruit of giant columnar cacti. Like hummingbirds, they hover in front of plants and insert their long noses and tongues deep into the flowers to sip nectar. In Texas, these bats occur in agave and desert-scrub woodlands at elevations of 4,900 to 7,500 feet. They are seldom found far from the agaves and cacti upon which they depend.

ROOSTING BEHAVIOR

They visit the Lone Star State only from June to August, and their numbers fluctuate widely from year to year. They roost in caves, abandoned mines, and cliff-face cavities in groups ranging from a few to several thousand. Many appear to make relatively long seasonal migrations, remaining active in warm climates year-round.

HUMAN ENCOUNTERS

These bats are seldom seen except at night at hummingbird feeders.

Vesper Bats
FAMILY VESPERTILIONIDAE

Pallid Bat (*Antrozous pallidus*) 23

Rafinesque's Big-eared Bat (*Corynorhinus rafinesquii*) 24

Townsend's Big-eared Bat (*Corynorhinus townsendii*) 26

Big Brown Bat (*Eptesicus fuscus*) 27

Spotted Bat (*Euderma maculatum*) 28

Silver-haired Bat (*Lasionycteris noctivagans*) 29

Western Red Bat (*Lasiurus blossevillii*) 30

Eastern Red Bat (*Lasiurus borealis*) 32

Hoary Bat (*Lasiurus cinereus*) 34

Southern Yellow Bat (*Lasiurus ega*) 35

Northern Yellow Bat (*Lasiurus intermedius*) 36

Seminole Bat (*Lasiurus seminolus*) 38

Western Yellow Bat (*Lasiurus xanthinus*) 39

Southeastern Myotis (*Myotis austroriparius*) 40

California Myotis (*Myotis californicus*) .42

Western Small-footed Myotis (*Myotis ciliolabrum*) 44

Little Brown Myotis (*Myotis lucifugus*) .46

Northern Myotis (*Myotis septentrionalis*) 48

Fringed Myotis (*Myotis thysanodes*) 50

Cave Myotis (*Myotis velifer*) 52

Long-legged Myotis (*Myotis volans*) 53

Yuma Myotis (*Myotis yumanensis*) 54

Evening Bat (*Nycticeius humeralis*) 56

Western Pipistrelle (*Pipistrellus hesperus*) 57

Eastern Pipistrelle (*Pipistrellus subflavus*) 58

Pallid Bat
Antrozous pallidus

ETYMOLOGY

Latin: *Antrozous* (cave animal);
Latin: *pallidus* (pale).

APPEARANCE

The fur of pallid bats is light brownish or grayish yellow on the back and cream or white on the belly. They are the only American bats whose fur on the back is distinctly lighter at the base than at the tip. They have large ears. Forearm: 1.9 to 2.3 inches (48 to 58 mm). Wingspan: 12.2 to 14.6 inches (310 to 370 mm).

MATING AND REARING YOUNG

After mating in October or November, sperm are stored until spring when females become pregnant. One or two babies are born in May or June.

HABITAT AND FOOD

Pallid bats live in arid grasslands and deserts and feed on virtually any large insect that is active at night near the ground. These include katydids, crickets, cicadas, large beetles, and moths. They also eat scorpions and even centipedes up to six inches long. Often injured while hunting such large and potentially dangerous prey, these bats recover quickly from broken bones, torn wing membranes, and wounds from thorns and cactus spines, even though they keep flying every night after the injury.

ROOSTING BEHAVIOR

Pallid bats roost in cliff-face crevices, tree hollows, beneath the bark of old snags, and in buildings and bridges. Nursery colonies typically include 30 to 150 females. Most pallid bats enter hibernation in late October or early November, apparently roosting in deep crevices in cliff faces until they emerge in March or April. Their "cave animal" name probably refers to their tendency to roost in caves and mines late at night while they digest their meal.

HUMAN ENCOUNTERS

Pallid bats often night-roost on residential porches, especially between 11 p.m. and 2 a.m. They also sometimes occupy bat houses that provide crevices 1.5 to 2 inches wide.

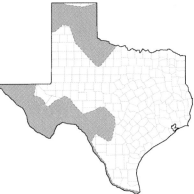

Rafinesque's Big-eared Bat (*Corynorhinus rafinesquii*)

Rafinesque's Big-eared Bat
Corynorhinus rafinesquii

© MERLIN D. TUTTLE, BCI \ 832-5104

ETYMOLOGY

Latin: *Corynorhinus* (club-nosed);
Latin: *rafinesquii* (named after C.S. Rafinesque).

APPEARANCE

Rafinesque's big-eared bats have very long ears. Large glands protrude from each side of the snout. The fur is grayish brown on the back and conspicuously bicolored with whitish tips on the belly. Forearm: 1.6 to 1.8 inches (40 to 46 mm). Wingspan: 10.4 to 11.9 inches (265 to 301 mm).

MATING AND REARING YOUNG

Mating is in late fall; one pup is born in late May or early June. Pups are capable of flight in three weeks and reach adult size in a month.

HABITAT AND FOOD

Rafinesque's big-eared bats live in lowland pine and hardwood forests. Moths appear to be their most common prey, though their diet also includes a variety of other insects, such as horseflies, crickets, and roaches.

ROOSTING BEHAVIOR

In Texas, Rafinesque's big-eared bats originally roosted primarily in the large hollows of exceptionally old trees. As old-growth forests have been cut, most remaining colonies have moved into unoccupied buildings, bridges, culverts, and wells. Due primarily to roost losses, the species is now considered threatened in Texas. Nursery colonies include up to 200 mothers with young. Within their coastal range, these bats remain active and feed year-round, falling into torpor only during the coldest weather.

HUMAN ENCOUNTERS

Humans most often encounter Rafinesque's big-eared bats in abandoned buildings.

Townsend's Big-eared Bat
Corynorhinus townsendii

© MERLIN D. TUTTLE, BCI \ 833-2203

ETYMOLOGY

Latin: *Corynorhinus* (club-nosed);
Latin: *townsendii* (named after Charles H. Townsend).

APPEARANCE

Townsend's big-eared bats have extremely long ears and distinct facial glands on either side of the nose. Their fur is long and uniformly pale to dark brown on the back and pinkish brown on the belly. Forearm: 1.5 to 1.9 inches (39 to 48 mm). Wingspan: 11.7 to 12.6 inches (297 to 320 mm).

MATING AND REARING YOUNG

Mating occurs from October to February; females give birth to a single pup between April and June.

HABITAT AND FOOD

Habitat ranges from coniferous forests, mixed forests, and deserts to stream and river areas of native prairies. They feed on small moths, beetles, flies, lacewings, dung beetles, and sawflies.

ROOSTING BEHAVIOR

Roosts are in caves or cave-like structures, such as mines and rock shelters. Nursery colonies typically include 150 or fewer adults, but can contain thousands. During winter, most Townsend's big-eared bats hibernate in cool, ventilated areas of caves or mines, where ambient temperatures are above freezing but below 53 degrees Fahrenheit.

HUMAN ENCOUNTERS

Townsend's big-eared bats are most often encountered by cavers, but colonies also can be found in barns and old abandoned buildings.

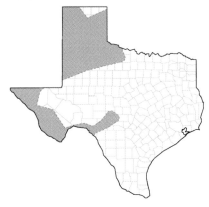

Big Brown Bat
Eptesicus fuscus

ETYMOLOGY

Greek: *Eptesicus* (flying);
Latin: *fuscus* (brown).

APPEARANCE

Big brown bats are robust, with a broad, sparsely furred nose. Fur is light copper to dark chocolate brown. Forearm: 1.7 to 2.0 inches (42 to 52 mm). Wingspan: 12.8 to 15.5 inches (325 to 393 mm).

MATING AND REARING YOUNG

Mating occurs in fall, but females store sperm until they ovulate in spring. In West Texas, females usually give birth to one pup in early summer; twins are common in eastern Texas.

HABITAT AND FOOD

Big brown bats often feed over wetlands, crops, parks, roadways, and around streetlights. Their diet includes ground beetles, June beetles, scarab beetles, leaf beetles, and spotted cucumber beetles, as well as stinkbugs, ants, leafhoppers, and caddis flies. In one summer, an average nursery colony of 150 big brown bats can easily eat 600,000 cucumber beetles, 194,000 scarab beetles, 335,000 stinkbugs, and 158,000 leafhoppers — all of them pests that damage crops and gardens. Though big brown bats thrive in a variety of habitats, they seem to prefer mature deciduous forests.

ROOSTING BEHAVIOR

In summer, females form nursery colonies of 25 to 75 individuals, while males live alone or in small bachelor groups. They roost in hollow oak and bald cypress trees, ponderosa pine snags, rock crevices, cave entrances, bridges, and buildings. Because big brown bats, unlike most other bat species, can survive subfreezing body temperatures, they can hibernate in many locations, including caves, rock crevices, tree hollows, bridge crevices, and buildings.

HUMAN ENCOUNTERS

Big brown bats, which frequently live in buildings year-round, are among the most commonly encountered bats in the state. They also readily occupy bat houses. In East Texas, they often are seen foraging around streetlights.

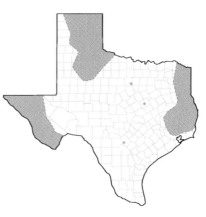

Spotted Bat
Euderma maculatum

© MERLIN D. TUTTLE, BCI \ 804-3303

ETYMOLOGY

Greek: *Euderma* (good skin);
Latin: *maculatum* (spotted).

APPEARANCE

Spotted bats have long, silky fur that is white on the belly and black on the back. The species is clearly distinguished by three large, white spots on the back and enormous pink ears. Forearm: 1.9 to 2.0 inches (48 to 51 mm). Wingspan: 13.6 to 14.4 inches (346 to 365 mm).

MATING AND REARING YOUNG

Mating is in fall; a single pup is born in June.

HABITAT AND FOOD

Spotted bats live in open desert areas, scrub country, and ponderosa pine forests. Distribution is patchy, at least partly because they apparently choose crevices in exceptionally tall cliff faces as their primary roosts. They feed mostly on small moths and, unlike most other bats, they emit distinctive, audible echolocation calls of such low frequency that the moths they prey upon have difficulty detecting them.

ROOSTING BEHAVIOR

Although no one has ever seen a spotted bat in its roost, radio-tracking studies clearly indicate that they are using crevices high up on cliff faces, where they appear to form small nursery colonies. They apparently remain in the same general areas year-round, moving deeper into crevices and becoming torpid during the most extreme winter weather. They emerge on all but the coldest nights and have been captured over ponds on subfreezing evenings.

HUMAN ENCOUNTERS

These bats are rarely seen except by researchers who net them as they fly over ponds to drink.

© MERLIN D. TUTTLE, BCI \ 807-4202

Silver-haired Bat
Lasionycteris noctivagans

ETYMOLOGY

Greek: *Lasionycteris* (hairy bat);
Latin: *noctivagans* (night wanderer).

APPEARANCE

Silver-haired bats have black or very dark brown fur that is silver-tipped. Unlike hoary bats, only the front half of its upper tail membrane is densely furred. Forearm: 1.5 to 1.7 inches (37 to 44 mm). Wingspan: 10.5 to 12.3 inches (266 to 313 mm).

MATING AND REARING YOUNG

Mating occurs mostly in fall, prior to migration, but females do not become pregnant until spring. They typically give birth to twins in June or July. The young apparently are raised primarily in Canada and the northern third of the United States, although pregnant females have been found in mountainous areas as far south as Arizona and Texas.

HABITAT AND FOOD

Silver-haired bats typically live in old-growth forests at relatively high elevations or in northern climates. Individuals occupy hunting territories that are often about 300 feet in diameter, and they feed on flies, midges, leafhoppers, moths, mosquitoes, beetles, true bugs, ants, and caddis flies.

ROOSTING BEHAVIOR

Silver-haired bats form nursery colonies that include from 10 to 70 individuals. They typically roost in woodpecker holes and other small tree cavities. Bachelors and migrating individuals are found behind loose bark, in woodpiles, in buildings, and sometimes in bridges. Most silver-haired bats migrate long distances and are seen in Texas only in fall, winter, or spring. In winter, they hibernate in deep rock crevices, tree cavities, and occasionally in cave entrances.

HUMAN ENCOUNTERS

Humans seldom encounter silver-haired bats, though a few individual bats sometimes enter woodpiles or buildings.

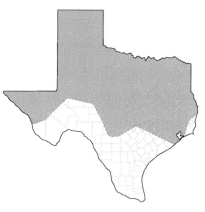

Western Red Bat (*Lasiurus blossevillii*)

Western Red Bat
Lasiurus blossevillii

ETYMOLOGY

Greek: *Lasiurus* (hairy tail);
Latin: *blossevillii* (rusty furred).

APPEARANCE

Western red bats have rather short, rounded ears. They are nearly indistinguishable from eastern red bats except through genetic comparison. Underarms are fully furred to the wrists, as are the first two-thirds of the tail membrane's upper surface. Contrasting white markings on the wrists and shoulders easily distinguish this species from yellow bats. Forearm: 1.3 to 1.7 inches (34 to 42 mm). Wingspan: 10.6 to 11.2 inches (270 to 285 mm).

MATING AND REARING YOUNG

Mating occurs in late summer and early fall. Litters of two to four pups are born, typically in the following June.

HABITAT AND FOOD

Western red bats live mostly along streams and rivers in thorn scrub and pine/oak forests where they feed on moths, true bugs, beetles, ants, and flies. The loss of lowland forests, mostly to agriculture and water-storage reservoirs, has greatly reduced both roosting and foraging habitat, and western red bats appear to be in potentially serious decline. The species is rare in Texas.

ROOSTING BEHAVIOR

Western red bats have been found roosting solitarily in the foliage of trees and shrubs adjacent to streams or open fields, in orchards, and sometimes in urban areas. The species is migratory and probably hibernates in locations similar to those chosen by its eastern relative, but its seasonal status in Texas is unknown.

HUMAN ENCOUNTERS

Humans seldom see this bat except when it feeds around street lamps. A few are found by fruit harvesters in orchards.

Eastern Red Bat (*Lasiurus borealis*)

© MERLIN D. TUTTLE, BCI \ 808-2300

Eastern Red Bat
Lasiurus borealis

ETYMOLOGY

Greek: *Lasiurus* (hairy tail); Latin: *borealis* (northern).

APPEARANCE

Eastern red bats have relatively short, rounded ears. The fur is reddish orange with a frosted appearance. Females, in contrast to the brightly colored males, are often lighter and grayer with only traces of red. Underarms are fully furred to the wrists, as is the upper surface of the tail membrane. Contrasting white markings on wrists and shoulders easily distinguish this species from yellow bats. Forearm: 1.5 to 1.8 inches (37 to 45 mm). Wingspan: 11.4 to 13.1 inches (290 to 332 mm).

MATING AND REARING YOUNG

Eastern red bats mate in August and September, often in flight. In early summer of the following year, females typically give birth to twins, triplets, or quadruplets — exceptionally large litters for bats.

HABITAT AND FOOD

Eastern red bats live in a wide variety of lowland forest habitats. They feed mostly on moths, but also on beetles, assassin bugs, planthoppers, leafhoppers, and spittlebugs.

ROOSTING BEHAVIOR

During summer, the bats roost in foliage, typically 18 to 40 feet above ground. They hang by one foot, wrapped in their furry tail membranes, and are well camouflaged, resembling dead leaves. Typically, eastern red bats live alone or in family groups consisting of a mother and her young. In Texas, they apparently remain in the same areas year-round. However, many red bats from farther north migrate into or through Texas in fall, although their exact destinations are unknown. In winter, they hibernate in various locations, ranging from tree hollows and exposed tree trunks to bunchgrass and leaf litter on the ground.

HUMAN ENCOUNTERS

Adults are most often seen feeding around streetlights. Mothers, weighted down by their pups, sometimes fall to the ground during storms and are found by people. You can help by gently moving them to a nearby branch, while wearing leather work gloves. Alternatively, a stick can be offered for the bats to hang onto, and the stick can be moved to a nearby tree or shrub.

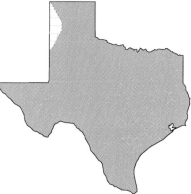

Hoary Bat
Lasiurus cinereus

© MERLIN D. TUTTLE, BCI \ 809-6200

ETYMOLOGY

Greek: *Lasiurus* (hairy tail);
Latin: *cinereus* (ash-colored).

APPEARANCE

Hoary bats have relatively short, rounded ears that are light-colored with a distinctive black edge. Their fur is distinct from all other species: The dark base is followed by a broad cream-colored band, then a slightly narrower band of mahogany, and finally a white tip. The result is a hoary or frosted appearance. The tail membrane is fully furred on top, as are the arms. As in red and Seminole bats, hoary bats have distinctive white patches on the shoulders and wrists. Forearm: 2.0 to 2.2 inches (50 to 57 mm). Wingspan: 13.3 to 16.7 inches (338 to 424 mm).

MATING AND REARING YOUNG

Mating occurs in fall; most females bear twins between mid-May and late June. Young resemble adults in 22 days and can fly well in 33 days.

HABITAT AND FOOD

Hoary bats occur in a wide variety of forested habitats, from sea level to high elevations. They feed mostly on moths, but also consume many other insects, from beetles to mosquitoes. They are highly territorial and return night after night to chosen feeding sites.

ROOSTING BEHAVIOR

Hoary bats are solitary, usually living alone or in family groups consisting of a mother and her young. They roost in the foliage of older trees at the edges of forests, close to pastures, fields, or clearings. This species is seen in Texas mostly during its spring and fall migrations. During hibernation, hoary bats have been found in Spanish moss, squirrel nests, woodpecker holes, and even in the open on tree trunks, where they rely on their unique fur color for extremely effective camouflage.

HUMAN ENCOUNTERS

Hoary bats are rarely encountered in Texas. Farther north, they are typically encountered when mothers fall to the ground with their young during storms.

Southern Yellow Bat
Lasiurus ega

ETYMOLOGY

Greek: *Lasiurus* (hairy tail);
Latin: *ega* (belonging to Ega [Brazil]).

APPEARANCE

Southern yellow bats have relatively short, rounded ears. Their fur is a dull, sooty yellow. Only the first half of the upper tail membrane is furred, and there are no distinctive white markings on wrists or shoulders. They are distinguished from northern yellow bats by their smaller size. Forearm: 1.7 to 1.9 inches (43 to 49 mm). Wingspan: 13.2 to 14.0 inches (335 to 355 mm).

MATING AND REARING YOUNG

Southern yellow bats mate in fall or early winter. Females give birth to two or three young between late April and July.

HABITAT AND FOOD

These bats' feeding habits remain unstudied, but they are assumed to rely on small- to medium-size flying insects. They are most often found among natural groves of palm trees along the Rio Grande near Brownsville, as well as in areas where ornamental palms have been planted.

ROOSTING BEHAVIOR

Southern yellow bats typically roost year-round beneath the hanging dead fronds of palm trees. The common practice of removing old palm fronds deprives the bats of roosting space and threatens their survival. Like their nearest relatives, these bats are probably nonmigratory, remaining active year-round except for brief periods of torpor during severe winter weather.

HUMAN ENCOUNTERS

Southern yellow bats are sometimes seen emerging from palm trees and are most often encountered when palm fronds are trimmed.

Northern Yellow Bat (*Lasiurus intermedius*)

Northern Yellow Bat
Lasiurus intermedius

ETYMOLOGY

Greek: *Lasiurus* (hairy tail);
Latin: *intermedius* (in the middle, central).

APPEARANCE

Northern yellow bats have relatively short, rounded ears. The fur ranges from yellowish orange or brown to nearly gray, often with slightly darker tips. Unlike red and hoary bats, only the front half of the upper tail membrane is furred, and there are no white markings on shoulders or wrists. The northern yellow bat is larger than the southern yellow bat. Forearm: 1.9 to 2.5 inches (47 to 63 mm). Wingspan: 13.8 to 17.2 inches (350 to 438 mm).

MATING AND REARING YOUNG

Mating occurs primarily in fall, probably in flight. Twins are typically born in late May or June.

HABITAT AND FOOD

Northern yellow bats live in a variety of mostly coastal habitats that contain Spanish moss or palm trees. They feed on leafhoppers, flies, mosquitoes, beetles, flying ants, and occasional damselflies and dragonflies.

ROOSTING BEHAVIOR

These bats roost year-round in Spanish moss or beneath the dead, hanging fronds of fan palms. Residential mosquito spraying appears to threaten this species, as does loss of Spanish moss and removal of old palm fronds. Northern yellow bats are nonmigratory and remain active year-round except for periods of extreme winter weather, during which they become torpid.

HUMAN ENCOUNTERS

Northern yellow bats may be seen at dusk, feeding around street lamps and over open areas such as golf courses.

Seminole Bat
Lasiurus seminolus

© MERLIN D. TUTTLE, BCI \ 812-1101

ETYMOLOGY

Greek: *Lasiurus* (hairy tail);
Latin: *seminolus* (belonging to Seminole [Native American tribe]).

APPEARANCE

Seminole bats have relatively short, rounded ears. Their fur is a distinctively deep mahogany color with frosted tips. The tail membrane is well furred to the tip of the tail. Fur extends along the underarms to the wrists and, as in red bats, there are distinctive white patches on the wrists and shoulders. Forearm: 1.4 to 1.8 inches (35 to 45 mm). Wingspan: approximately 11.8 inches (300 mm).

MATING AND REARING YOUNG

It is assumed that mating occurs in late fall or early winter. Most litters consist of two to four pups born in late May or early June. Young are fully furred and almost identical to their mothers by the time they are two weeks old. They can fly in three to four weeks.

HABITAT AND FOOD

Seminole bats are closely associated with lowland, wooded areas that support Spanish moss. They feed mostly along forest edges on moths, leafhoppers, flies, beetles, ants, and crickets.

ROOSTING BEHAVIOR

These bats roost, usually alone, in tree foliage and in Spanish moss 6 to 12 feet above the ground. They appear to be nonmigratory, entering torpor during extreme winter weather but emerging to feed on the warmest evenings.

HUMAN ENCOUNTERS

Spanish moss collectors regularly encounter Seminole bats. Otherwise, they are usually seen only as they feed around streetlights.

Western Yellow Bat
Lasiurus xanthinus

ETYMOLOGY

Greek: *Lasiurus* (hairy tail);
Greek: *xanthinus* (yellowish).

APPEARANCE

Western yellow bats have short, rounded ears and yellowish fur. Only the front half of the upper tail membrane is furred. These bats cannot be distinguished from southern yellow bats without genetic testing. Forearm: 1.8 to 1.9 inches (45 to 48 mm). Wingspan: 13.2 to 14.0 inches (335 to 355 cm).

MATING AND REARING YOUNG

Little is known about the mating behavior of western yellow bats. Mating is presumed to occur in fall, with one to four pups born in May or June.

HABITAT AND FOOD

Western yellow bats occur in desert regions of the southwestern U.S. and adjacent Mexico. They feed on a variety of small insects, their diet probably resembling that of the similar southern yellow bat.

ROOSTING BEHAVIOR

Western yellow bats live solitarily in the skirts of dead fronds of both native and non-native palm trees, as well as in yucca plants and the foliage of hackberry and sycamore trees. Their roosting choices during extreme winter weather remain unknown, but like their nearest relatives, they probably are nonmigratory and enter torpor. They emerge and feed on warm evenings year-round.

HUMAN ENCOUNTERS

In Texas, western yellow bats have been reported only in the Big Bend region and are rarely seen by people.

Southeastern Myotis (*Myotis austroriparius*)

Southeastern Myotis
Myotis austroriparius

ETYMOLOGY

Latin: *Myotis* (mouse ear);
Latin: *austroriparius* (southern stream banks).

APPEARANCE

Southeastern myotis have short, thick, woolly fur, which is distinctly bicolored. On the back, the fur is darker at the base with russet or dark gray tips, while fur on the belly is black at the base with white or whitish tips. Forearm: 1.3 to 1.7 inches (33 to 42 mm). Wingspan: 9.4 to 10.6 inches (238 to 270 mm).

MATING AND REARING YOUNG

In southern areas, most mating occurs in late winter or early spring; females give birth in late April or early May, usually to twins.

HABITAT AND FOOD

Southeastern myotis live in lowland oak/hickory and mixed conifer/hardwood forests, where they feed on midges, mosquitoes, small moths, beetles, and crane flies.

ROOSTING BEHAVIOR

Nursery colonies are found mostly in hollow gum trees, but also in culverts, bridges, buildings, bat houses, caves, and mines. In Texas, southeastern myotis hibernate in tightly packed clusters in hollow trees and occasionally in culverts or bridges. In other Gulf States, they also use caves and abandoned mines. They spend winters in the vicinity of their summer territories and emerge to feed on warm evenings.

HUMAN ENCOUNTERS

With a strong flashlight, southeastern myotis can be observed foraging low over lakes and rivers. They are occasionally found in buildings.

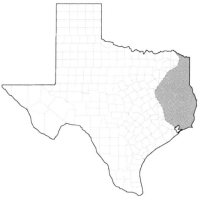

California Myotis (*Myotis californicus*)

© MERLIN D. TUTTLE, BCI \ 861-3206

California Myotis
Myotis californicus

ETYMOLOGY

Latin: *Myotis* (mouse ear);
Latin: *californicus* (belonging to California).

APPEARANCE

California myotis are similar in size to the western small-footed myotis. They have dark brown ears and wing membranes, a dark facial mask, and light reddish-brown fur. Feet are tiny, very similar to those of the western small-footed myotis, which is distinguishable only by experts. Forearm: 1.1 to 1.4 inches (29 to 36 mm). Wingspan: approximately 9.1 inches (230 mm).

MATING AND REARING YOUNG

California myotis mate in fall and give birth to a single pup in June or July.

HABITAT AND FOOD

They are common inhabitants of desert valleys and badlands, especially near water. They feed on small insects, including moths, flies, and beetles.

ROOSTING BEHAVIOR

California myotis form nursery colonies of 2 to 25 mothers, mostly in cliff-face crevices, tree cavities, and buildings. They probably enter torpor in deep rock crevices during the coldest winter weather, though some have been found, either alone or in small groups, in caves, mines, and buildings. At least some emerge to feed on warm evenings.

HUMAN ENCOUNTERS

Small colonies of California myotis have been found roosting in buildings, though this is rare.

Western Small-footed Myotis (*Myotis ciliolabrum*)

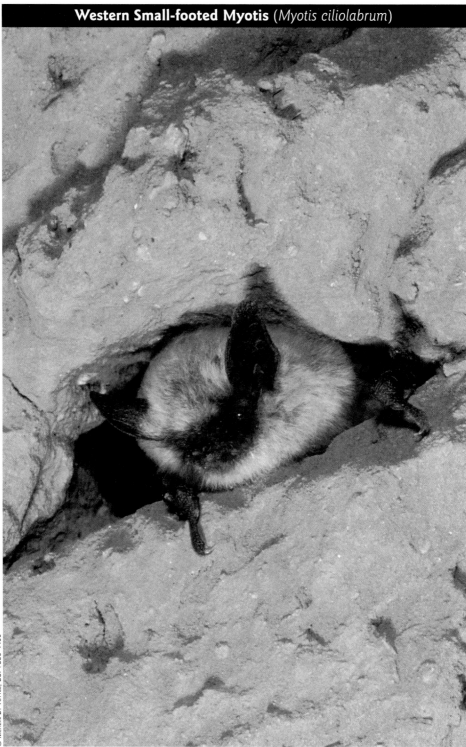

Western Small-footed Myotis
Myotis ciliolabrum

© MERLIN D. TUTTLE, BCI \ 850-4100

ETYMOLOGY

Latin: *Myotis* (mouse ear);
Latin: *ciliolabrum* (hairy lips).

APPEARANCE

Western small-footed myotis are buff-brown bats with black ears, a black mask across the eyes and nose, and, as the common name implies, tiny feet. This species can be distinguished from the California myotis only by experts. Forearm: 1.1 to 1.4 inches (29 to 36 mm). Wingspan: 8.1 to 9.8 inches (205 to 248 mm).

MATING AND REARING YOUNG

Mating occurs in fall, with births from late May through early July. Litter size appears to vary regionally, with mothers typically producing just one pup each, but sometimes twins.

HABITAT AND FOOD

Western small-footed myotis are typically found near water in wooded mountainous regions, including the chaparral forests of the Trans-Pecos and Palo Duro Canyon areas. These bats seem to prefer small moths, but also catch midges, caddis flies, crane flies, small beetles, true bugs, leafhoppers, and flying ants.

ROOSTING BEHAVIOR

Nursery colonies include from 2 to 25 mothers and young and are typically located in erosion cavities, rock crevices, or under loose tree bark. They also have been found in bridges and buildings. Hibernation sites have not been found in Texas, but are probably located in deep rock crevices.

HUMAN ENCOUNTERS

Western small-footed myotis are rarely seen by people.

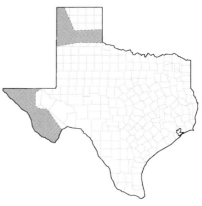

Little Brown Myotis (*Myotis lucifugus*)

Little Brown Myotis
Myotis lucifugus

© MERLIN D. TUTTLE, BCI \ 828-1500

ETYMOLOGY

Latin: *Myotis* (mouse ear);
Latin: *lucifugus* (fleeing light).

APPEARANCE

Little brown myotis have long, glossy fur that varies in color, ranging from pale tan to dark chocolate on the back and slightly lighter on the belly. Forearm: 1.3 to 1.6 inches (34 to 41 mm). Wingspan: 8.7 to 10.6 inches (222 to 269 mm).

MATING AND REARING YOUNG

Mating typically occurs in fall. Each female gives birth to one pup between May and early July. The young are able to fly about 24 days after birth.

HABITAT AND FOOD

The little brown myotis has been documented only once in Texas, in the Trans-Pecos region. It is common in other areas of the United States, except for the Plains states. It lives and feeds along rivers and streams, eating emerging aquatic insects such as midges, mayflies, mosquitoes, and caddis flies, as well as small moths and beetles.

ROOSTING BEHAVIOR

These bats roost in rock crevices, caves, mines, old buildings, bridges, culverts, and bat houses. Tree roosts also include locations under bark, in snags, or within woodpecker holes. Nursery colonies can include 20 to 30,000 or more individuals. They frequently rest in night roosts to digest their meals before flying out to forage again. In the eastern United States, this species migrates long distances to hibernate in caves and mines, often in colonies numbering a million or more. Little is known about hibernation requirements in the western U.S.

HUMAN ENCOUNTERS

In areas where they are common, little brown myotis are often found in buildings and bat houses, but they are rarely encountered in Texas.

Northern Myotis (*Myotis septentrionalis*)

Northern Myotis
Myotis septentrionalis

ETYMOLOGY

Latin: *Myotis* (mouse ear);
Latin: *septentrionalis* (northern).

APPEARANCE

Northern myotis have dull, grayish-brown fur that is lighter on the belly. Their ears are long compared to most other myotis. Forearm: 1.3 to 1.5 inches (32 to 39 mm). Wingspan: 9.0 to 10.2 inches (228 to 258 mm).

MATING AND REARING YOUNG

Mating occurs in the fall, before hibernation; females give birth in June or July to a single pup. The young are capable of flight in about three weeks.

HABITAT AND FOOD

This species has only been found once in Texas. It lives in forested areas from the southeastern U.S. through northwestern Canada. Northern long-eared myotis feed in forests, below the canopy level and often near the ground. They are very maneuverable fliers and can snatch moths directly from vegetation. Moths are the main prey, but caddis flies, leafhoppers, mayflies, small beetles, and lacewings are also eaten occasionally.

ROOSTING BEHAVIOR

Nursery colonies are found mostly in large, old trees, under loose bark, and in buildings. Some occupy bat houses. They hibernate in small groups in caves and mines.

HUMAN ENCOUNTERS

Small colonies are most likely to be seen in bat houses or attics.

Fringed Myotis (*Myotis thysanodes*)

Fringed Myotis
Myotis thysanodes

ETYMOLOGY

Latin: *Myotis* (mouse ear);
Greek: *thysanodes* (with a fringe).

APPEARANCE

Fringed myotis have relatively long ears and long, reddish-brown fur. A conspicuous fringe of hair along the rear edge of the tail membrane distinguishes this species from all others. Forearm: 1.6 to 1.9 inches (40 to 47 mm). Wingspan: 10.4 to 11.8 inches (265 to 300 mm).

MATING AND REARING YOUNG

Mating takes place in fall; females give birth to one pup each in June or early July. Juveniles are sometimes proficient fliers 20 days after birth.

HABITAT AND FOOD

Fringed myotis live in desert scrublands, grasslands, and oak and pine/juniper woodlands, often near water. They feed mostly on beetles and moths.

ROOSTING BEHAVIOR

Fringed myotis roost in caves, abandoned mines, rock crevices in cliff faces, old buildings, and bridges. Nursery colonies include 10 to 2,000 individuals. Hibernating fringed myotis have been found in buildings and underground mines. They have not been found in Texas in winter, but probably are year-round residents that retreat into deep cliff-face crevices and enter extended torpor during cold weather.

HUMAN ENCOUNTERS

Fringed myotis only occasionally enter buildings and are seldom encountered by people.

Cave Myotis
Myotis velifer

© Merlin D. Tuttle, BCI \ 856-2504

ETYMOLOGY

Latin: *Myotis* (mouse ear);
Latin: *velifer* (bearing a veil).

APPEARANCE

Cave myotis have light brown or grayish fur and a stub-by-nosed appearance. This is the largest myotis within its range. It lacks the distinguishing characteristics of its nearest relatives, such as extra-long ears, white-tipped belly fur, a black mask on its face, or a keeled calcar (a bony spur attached to the ankle). Forearm: 1.5 to 1.9 inches (38 to 47 mm). Wingspan: 11.0 to 12.4 inches (280 to 315 mm).

MATING AND REARING YOUNG

These bats mate from late September to March. At the end of April and in early May, Texas females give birth to a single pup, which learns to fly in just three weeks.

HABITAT AND FOOD

Cave myotis live in a wide variety of habitats, most often near waterways in arid or semiarid areas. They feed on moths, weevils, ant lions, beetles, and other small insects.

ROOSTING BEHAVIOR

These bats roost in rock crevices, caves, old buildings, bridges, culverts, and bat houses. Nursery colonies can include from dozens of individuals to 15,000 or more. Roosts are frequently shared with Mexican free-tailed bats. Cave myotis are permanent Texas residents that migrate over relatively short distances to find caves that trap enough cool air to permit winter hibernation.

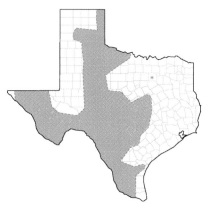

HUMAN ENCOUNTERS

Cave myotis readily occupy bat houses and sometimes live in buildings. Thousands of these bats often share cave roosts with Mexican free-tailed bats, typically emerging after most of the Mexican free-tailed bats have left. Cave myotis can be recognized by their more erratic flight, which is typically nearer the ground.

© MERLIN D. TUTTLE, BCI \ 853-5201

Long-legged Myotis
Myotis volans

ETYMOLOGY

Latin: *Myotis* (mouse ear);
Latin: *volans* (flying).

APPEARANCE

Long-legged myotis have dark brown or grayish fur; short, rounded ears; and a keeled calcar. Unlike other myotis bats, their long, dense fur extends along the underside of the wing membranes to a line from the elbows to the knees. Forearm: 1.4 to 1.7 inches (35 to 42 mm). Wingspan: 9.8 to 10.6 inches (250 to 270 mm).

MATING AND REARING YOUNG

Mating typically occurs in fall; one pup is born to each female in June or early July.

HABITAT AND FOOD

Long-legged myotis live in coniferous forests and tall, open woods of mountainous areas, although they can also be found seasonally along streams in desert habitats. They frequently feed on moths and other soft-bodied insects, but also eat beetles, flies, true bugs, and leafhoppers.

ROOSTING BEHAVIOR

These bats roost in cliff-face crevices, under loose tree bark, in tree cavities, and sometimes in abandoned buildings. Nursery colonies can include up to several hundred mothers. Most long-legged myotis seem to simply disappear in winter. Some hibernate in caves and mine tunnels, with the remainder most likely retreating into deep rock crevices.

HUMAN ENCOUNTERS

Long-legged myotis are seldom encountered by people.

Long-legged Myotis (*Myotis volans*)

Yuma Myotis (*Myotis yumanensis*)

Yuma Myotis
Myotis yumanensis

ETYMOLOGY

Latin: *Myotis* (mouse ear);
Latin: *yumanensis* (belonging to Yuma [Arizona]).

APPEARANCE

Yuma myotis have gray or brown to pale tan fur on the back and white or whitish fur on the belly. Forearm: 1.3 to 1.5 inches (32 to 38 mm). Wingspan: approximately 9.3 inches (235 mm).

MATING AND REARING YOUNG

Mating typically occurs in fall; each female gives birth to one pup between May and early July.

HABITAT AND FOOD

Yuma myotis are common in summer in the Rio Grande and southern Trans-Pecos areas, where they live and feed along rivers and cottonwood-lined streams. They eat emerging aquatic insects such as caddis flies, midges, and mosquitoes, as well as small moths, beetles, froghoppers, and leafhoppers. They are efficient feeders and can fill their stomachs in 15 to 20 minutes.

ROOSTING BEHAVIOR

These bats roost in cliff crevices, caves, mines, tunnels, bridges, and buildings. Females form nursery colonies of up to several thousand individuals. They frequently rest in night roosts to digest their meals before flying out to forage again. At least short, seasonal migrations probably occur, accompanied by extended periods of torpor, perhaps deep in cliff-face crevices.

HUMAN ENCOUNTERS

Yuma myotis often roost in buildings.

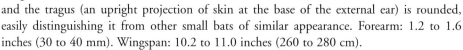

Evening Bat
Nycticeius humeralis

© MERLIN D. TUTTLE, BCI \ 831-1201

ETYMOLOGY

Greek: *Nycticeius* (belonging to the night);
Latin: *humeralis* (pertaining to the humerus).

APPEARANCE

Evening bats are small and dark brown with black wings, ears, and nose. Fur on the back is bicolored, and the tragus (an upright projection of skin at the base of the external ear) is rounded, easily distinguishing it from other small bats of similar appearance. Forearm: 1.2 to 1.6 inches (30 to 40 mm). Wingspan: 10.2 to 11.0 inches (260 to 280 cm).

MATING AND REARING YOUNG

Mating occurs in fall, possibly during migration; females give birth in late May or early June to twins. Juvenile males leave the nursery roost once they are weaned, but females apparently remain with their mothers for life.

HABITAT AND FOOD

Evening bats live in deciduous and coniferous bottomland forests, where they are most often found along water courses. Their diet is mostly beetles such as carabid, cucumber, Japanese, and June beetles. They also eat flying ants, spittlebugs, pomace flies, stinkbugs, and small moths. Research on a colony of 300 evening bats documented that they consumed approximately 63 million insects per summer, primarily spotted cucumber beetles — a costly pest to vine plants and corn crops.

ROOSTING BEHAVIOR

Roosts are in tree cavities, behind loose bark, in buildings, and in bat houses. Females form nursery colonies of 25 to 1,000 individuals, and they often share roosts with other species,

especially Mexican free-tailed bats. This species is migratory in the northern parts of its range, but appears to remain in one area in milder climates of the South. Northern migrants probably pass through or remain in Texas during the winter. Their winter roosts remain undiscovered but are probably in tree hollows; at least some evening bats emerge from their roosts on warm evenings.

HUMAN ENCOUNTERS

Evening bats frequently occur in buildings and bat houses where their evening emergences are easily observed.

Western Pipistrelle
Pipistrellus hesperus

ETYMOLOGY

Italian: *Pipistrellus* (bat);
Latin: *hesperus* (western).

APPEARANCE

Western pipistrelles are the smallest of all North American bats. The fur is light gray to yellowish, but the short, rounded ears and face are nearly black. This creates a sharply contrasting, mask-like appearance. Wing and tail membranes are also very dark. This bat is easily distinguished from California and small-footed myotis by its curved and blunt — rather than pointed — tragus. Forearm: 1.0 to 1.3 inches (26 to 33 mm). Wingspan: 7.5 to 8.5 inches (190 to 215 mm).

MATING AND REARING YOUNG

Mating occurs in late September and early October, with sperm apparently stored in the female reproductive tract until ovulation in spring. Females give birth to twins in late May or June.

HABITAT AND FOOD

Western pipistrelles are one of the most common bats in the Desert Southwest. They are especially abundant in deep, rocky canyons, where they feed on such small swarming insects as flying ants, mosquitoes, flies, leafhoppers, moths, beetles, caddis flies, stone flies, leafbugs, and spittlebugs.

ROOSTING BEHAVIOR

Most western pipistrelles roost in cliff-face crevices and under rocks. In some areas, they may resort to rodent burrows, and a few have been found in buildings. They are believed to make only short, seasonal movements. Hibernation occurs in deep, rock crevices, though a few use caves and mines. Some emerge to drink, even on subfreezing evenings.

HUMAN ENCOUNTERS

Western pipistrelles are often the first bats seen at dusk, sometimes more than an hour before sundown. As the sun sets, they can be seen feeding over streams and ponds of the Trans-Pecos region. Stray individuals occasionally are found in buildings.

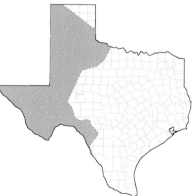

Eastern Pipistrelle
Pipistrellus subflavus

© Merlin D. Tuttle, BCI \ 832-1502

Etymology

Italian: *Pipistrellus* (bat);
Latin: *subflavus* (yellow belly).

Appearance

The eastern pipistrelle is one of the state's smallest bats. It is yellowish brown with black wing membranes surrounding bright reddish-orange forearms. When parted, the fur along the back is distinctly tricolored — in contrast to other small species. Ears are short and rounded, and the tragus is blunt. Forearm: 1.2 to 1.4 inches (31 to 36 mm). Wingspan: 8.2 to 10.2 inches (208 to 258 mm).

Mating and Rearing Young

Mating occurs in autumn before hibernation and, in some cases, again in spring; females store sperm until they ovulate in spring. Twins are born from late May to mid-July, with the two pups together weighing nearly half the mother's body weight.

Habitat and Food

Eastern pipistrelles live in forested lowlands. They hunt small insects, including leafhoppers, beetles, flies, moths, and flying ants in a variety of habitats throughout their range. They feed over waterways, ponds, and along forest edges, sometimes catching an insect every two seconds.

Roosting Behavior

In summer, males are often solitary, while females form nursery colonies of up to 35 individuals in tree foliage and occasionally in buildings. In East Texas, these bats apparently make only short trips to their winter hibernation sites, most of which may be in tree hollows; so far, however, they have only been found hibernating in highway culverts in the eastern part of the state. In Central Texas, eastern pipistrelles frequently roost in caves.

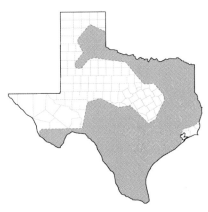

Human Encounters

Solitary eastern pipistrelles are occasionally spotted roosting in or on buildings.

Free-tailed Bats
FAMILY MOLOSSIDAE

Greater Bonneted Bat (*Eumops perotis*) 60

Pocketed Free-tailed Bat (*Nyctinomops femorosaccus*) 61

Big Free-tailed Bat (*Nyctinomops macrotis*) 62

Mexican Free-tailed Bat (*Tadarida brasiliensis*) 64

Greater Bonneted Bat
Eumops perotis

© MERLIN D. TUTTLE, BCI \ 806-2501

ETYMOLOGY

Greek: *Eumops* (good bat);
Greek: *perotis* (maimed ear).

APPEARANCE

Greater bonneted bats are the largest bats in the United States. At least a third of the tail extends past the tail membrane. Large, broad ears slant forward and extend beyond the tip of the nose, possibly providing additional lift in flight. Unlike other Texas free-tails, this species has no wrinkles on the lips. Forearm: 2.9 to 3.2 inches (73 to 82 mm). Wingspan: 20.9 to 22.4 inches (530 to 570 mm).

MATING AND REARING YOUNG

Mating occurs in spring; one pup is usually born in June or July.

HABITAT AND FOOD

Greater bonneted bats live in desert, chaparral, oak woodlands, and open ponderosa pine forests, always in close association with cliffs. They feed on a wide variety of insects, including grasshoppers, cicadas, crickets, moths, beetles, flies, and leafbugs.

ROOSTING BEHAVIOR

Roosts are in cliff-face crevices high up the walls of rugged, rocky canyons. Colonies typically include fewer than 100 individuals, with dominant males sharing the roosts with females year-round. They are not known to migrate. Brief periods of extreme weather are survived by entering torpor.

HUMAN ENCOUNTERS

The greater bonneted bat's loud echolocation calls are easily audible to humans and can be heard along desert river valleys, especially where cliffs are nearby. These bats can be observed in flight by using a powerful spotlight. They occasionally try to live in buildings, where they are easily heard and detected.

© MERLIN D. TUTTLE, BCI \ 858-1502

Pocketed Free-tailed Bat
Nyctinomops femorosaccus

ETYMOLOGY

Greek: *Nyctinomops* (night bat);
Latin: *femorosaccus* (sac on the thigh).

APPEARANCE

Pocketed free-tailed bats have tails that extend at least a third of their length beyond the tail membrane. Wings are long and narrow, and fur is dark brown to gray. Their lips show vertical wrinkles, similar to those of Mexican free-tailed bats. Unlike Mexican free-tails, however, their broad, round ears are joined at the base. The name comes from a shallow fold of skin on the underside of the tail membrane, near the knee, which forms a tiny pocket. Forearm: 1.7 to 2.0 inches (44 to 50 mm). Wingspan: 12.8 to 14.2 inches (325 to 360 mm).

MATING AND REARING YOUNG

Mating occurs in spring; one pup is born in late June or July.

HABITAT AND FOOD

Pocketed free-tailed bats live in arid desert areas and feed on moths, flying ants, leafhoppers, crickets, stinkbugs, and lacewings.

ROOSTING BEHAVIOR

These bats roost year-round in crevices high on cliff faces of rugged canyons. Nursery colonies are relatively small, usually including fewer than 100 individuals.

HUMAN ENCOUNTERS

Pocketed free-tailed bats are rarely encountered by humans.

Big Free-tailed Bat (*Nyctinomops macrotis*)

Big Free-tailed Bat
Nyctinomops macrotis

ETYMOLOGY

Greek: *Nyctinomops* (night bat);
Greek: *macrotis* (large ear).

APPEARANCE

Big free-tailed bats have exceptionally long, narrow wings relative to body size, and their tails extend past the tail membrane for at least a third of the membrane's length. Like Mexican free-tails, they have vertical wrinkles on their upper lips. Large, round ears are joined at the base, as in pocketed free-tails. Fur is reddish to dark brown or gray. This bat is much larger than any other species that has vertically wrinkled lips and is exceeded in size only by mastiff bats, whose lips are not wrinkled. Forearm: 2.3 to 2.5 inches (58 to 64 mm). Wingspan: 16.3 to 17.2 inches (413 to 436 mm).

MATING AND REARING YOUNG

After mating in spring, one pup is born in June or July.

HABITAT AND FOOD

Big free-tailed bats typically live in desert and arid grassland areas where there are rocky outcrops, canyons, or cliffs. They feed mostly on moths, but also on crickets, flying ants, stinkbugs, leafhoppers, and froghoppers.

ROOSTING BEHAVIOR

Big free-tailed bats roost in rock crevices high on cliff faces, and occasionally in buildings. Nursery colonies range in size from 20 to 150 individuals. Limited observations indicate that these bats migrate south into Mexico in October and return in May.

HUMAN ENCOUNTERS

The low-frequency echolocation calls of big free-tailed bats are easily audible to humans. The bats are seldom encountered by people, though they can often be heard calling high overhead in cliff-sided river valleys of the Big Bend area. Such bats can be briefly observed with the aid of a powerful spotlight, often in association with larger mastiff bats.

Mexican Free-tailed Bat (*Tadarida brasiliensis*)

Mexican Free-tailed Bat
Tadarida brasiliensis

ETYMOLOGY

Latin: *Tadarida* (withered toad);
Latin: *brasiliensis* (belonging to Brazil).

APPEARANCE

Mexican free-tailed bats have long, narrow wings; their tails extend beyond the tail membrane for about a third of its length. Fur is gray in new molt, then fades to rusty brown. They have large, rounded ears and vertical wrinkles on their upper lips. Forearm: 1.5 to 1.8 inches (38 to 46 mm). Wingspan: 11.3 to 13.4 inches (287 to 340 mm).

MATING AND REARING YOUNG

Mating occurs in March and April. After a gestation period of approximately 11 weeks, each mother bears a single pup, usually in June.

HABITAT AND FOOD

These bats occupy a broad range of habitats, from deserts to pine/oak forests and piñon/juniper woodlands, and rank among Texas' most ecologically and economically important animals. An estimated 100 million live in the Hill Country alone, where each million bats consume about 10 tons of insects nightly. They feed on a variety of prey, including moths, beetles, flying ants, leafhoppers, midges, mosquitoes, water boatmen, and green lacewings. Each night from spring to early summer, they catch billions of migrating moth pests, especially corn earworm, army and tobacco budworm moths, sparing farmers millions of dollars in crop losses.

ROOSTING BEHAVIOR

Most Mexican free-tailed bats roost in caves, but many live in abandoned mines and in tunnels, buildings, bridges, bat houses, and cliff-face crevices. Nursery colonies can contain hundreds to millions of bats. (Bracken Cave, near San Antonio, hosts about 20 million Mexican free-tailed bats — the largest aggregation of warm-blooded animals on Earth.) Most of these bats migrate to Mexico for the winter and begin returning to Texas nursery sites in early March. Thousands of these bats remain in Texas year-round, entering torpor during winter extremes, but emerging to feed on warm evenings.

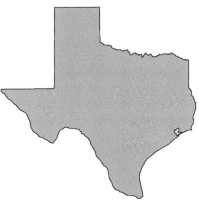

HUMAN ENCOUNTERS

Mexican free-tailed bats are the most commonly encountered bats in Texas, and their spectacular evening emergences are easily observed (see page 66). They are often seen around street lamps, and they readily occupy bat houses.

Bat Watching in Texas

© MERLIN D. TUTTLE, BCI \ 876-5502

Bracken Cave

The bats of Bracken Cave, the largest bat colony in the world, are an awe-inspiring sight when they emerge in the evenings.

Bracken Cave

The world's largest community of mammals — some 20 million Mexican free-tailed bats — roosts each summer in Bracken Cave, just north of San Antonio. Their evening emergences, which can last three hours, are among the most awesome sights in nature. After leaving the cave, the bats spread over thousands of square miles of surrounding farms and towns and consume more than 200 tons of insects nightly.

This critical bat habitat and the enormous colony are being conserved by Bat Conservation International, which purchased the cave in 1992. To protect the site, visits currently are limited to BCI members and special guests on a few scheduled evenings each year. BCI plans to develop a bat-education center and public viewing facility at the cave.

Congress Avenue Bridge

The Congress Avenue Bridge in Austin, about a mile south of the state capitol, is home to 1.5 million Mexican free-tailed bats — the largest urban bat colony in North America. Their evening emergences offer some of the world's most spectacular bat-watching opportunities.

For best viewing, watch from the bridge or from the *Austin American-Statesman* newspaper's Bat Observation Center. Or you may wish to watch from a tour boat from Capital Cruises or the Lone Star Riverboat. Several restaurants and hotels on Town Lake have outside decks for bat viewing.

Interesting bat flights can be seen from March to November, but they are reliably spectacular nearly every evening only in August, especially near the middle of the month. At other times, the emergence is highly influenced by weather and the bats often leave only after it is too dark to see them well. For emergence times, call the Bat Conservation International Bat Hotline at 512-416-5700, category 3636, or visit www.batcon.org.

Clarity Tunnel

The Clarity Tunnel is in Caprock Canyons State Park in the Texas Panhandle, east of Silverton, in Briscoe County. The abandoned railroad tunnel, about 700 feet long and 4.5 miles from the main parking area, is home to a colony of several hundred thousand Mexican free-tailed bats. For details about the site, including a map, contact the park at 806-455-1492, or visit www.tpwd.state.tx.us/park/caprock/caprock.htm.

Devil's Sinkhole State Natural Area

The Devil's Sinkhole is near Rocksprings, some 50 miles northeast of Kickapoo Cavern. Approximately one million Mexican free-tailed bats leave the 150-foot-deep cave every evening during the summer and fall. The 60-foot-wide column of bats is a spectacular sight. The park is closed to the public except by guided tour during the months bats are present. Tours are $8 for adults and $4 for children under 12. For more information and reservations, contact Kickapoo Cavern State Park, Box 705, Brackettville, TX 78832; 830-563-2342, or visit www.tpwd.state.tx.us/park/sinkhole/sinkhole.htm.

Eckert James River Bat Cave

The Eckert James River Bat Cave is located about 18 miles southwest of Mason, off Ranch Road 2389. This unique reserve, one of the top 10 Mexican free-tailed bat sites in the United States, is jointly managed by Bat Conservation International and The Nature Conservancy of Texas (TNC). After pups are born in early June, this limestone cave is home to an estimated six million bats. The reserve is open, and interpretive tours are available, from 6 p.m. to 9 p.m., Thursday through Sunday, from mid-May to mid-October. Group tours can be arranged

© KAREN MARKS, BCI \ 907-6501

Congress Avenue Bridge

The largest urban bat colony in the world — up to 1.5 million Mexican free-tailed bats — spends summer and fall under the Congress Avenue Bridge in downtown Austin.

© MERLIN D. TUTTLE, BCI \ 837-4101

Frio Cave

Monday through Wednesday. Admission is free. The cave is not wheelchair-accessible. For more information, contact the TNC at P.O. Box 164255, Austin, TX 78716; 512-263-8878; or visit www.tnc.org/texas/profiles/bat.htm.

Frio Cave

Frio Cave, located near Garner State Park, is home to Texas' second-largest free-tail colony, with peak populations estimated at 10 to 12 million. The viewing area is on the Annandale Ranch, about six miles southeast of Concan, Texas. Escorted tours are conducted Friday and Saturday evenings, Memorial Day weekend through Labor Day weekend. Group tours of 20 or more may be scheduled for other nights by special arrangement. Admission is $5 for adults; children under 13 are admitted free. For more information or to schedule groups, call Bill Cofer at 830-988-2864, or e-mail bpcofer0420@yahoo.com.

Old Tunnel Wildlife Management Area

The Old Tunnel Wildlife Management Area is located between Fredericksburg and Comfort, near the Old San Antonio Road. A free public-viewing deck is available seven days a week. At peak season, in late summer and early fall, up to two million Mexican free-tailed bats can be seen departing each evening from the historic 920-foot-long Fredericksburg & Northern Railroad tunnel. Bat-watching tours are offered on Thursdays and Saturdays from June through October. The tours, which are conducted on a first-come, first-served basis, are free for families with a Texas Conservation Passport or Limited Public Use or Annual Public Hunt permit; fees for other visitors are $5 for adults, $2 for children age 6 to 16, and $3 for seniors. For additional information, contact the LBJ State Historical Park at 830-644-2478: or visit www.tpwd.state.tx.us/wma/wmarea/tunnel.htm#text.

Stuart Bat Cave

Stuart Bat Cave (formerly Green Cave) is in the Kickapoo Cavern State Park, 22.5 miles north of Brackettville on Ranch Road 674. The park offers bat-watching tours to view the emergence of up to one million Mexican free-tailed bats. Tours are available from late April through October, but Kickapoo is a restricted-access park: Appointments must be made prior to visiting. Admission is $2, and bat tours are an additional $5 for adults and $3 for children under 13. For more information and reservations, contact Kickapoo Cavern State Park, Box 705, Brackettville, TX 78832; 830-563-2342; or visit www.tpwd.state.tx.us/park/kickapoo/kickapoo.htm.

Books about Bats

For Children

Bash, B. 1993. *Shadows of the Night*. Sierra Club Books for Children, San Francisco, CA, 30 pp. With easy-to-read text and glowing watercolors, the author paints a lovely picture of a year in the life of a little brown bat, dispelling the mystery that surrounds these harmless and beneficial creatures. For grades 2-5.

Bauld, J. 1998. *Hector's Escapades: The First Night Out*. Eakin Publications, Austin, TX, 39 pp. This charming books tells the story of a Mexican free-tailed bat who learns the nightly bug-catching routine for the bats that live under the Congress Avenue bridge in Austin, TX. For grades K-2.

Cannon, J. 1993. *Stellaluna*. Harcourt, Brace, & Company, New York, NY, 48 pp. This beautifully illustrated volume tells the imaginative story of a young fruit bat separated from her mother and raised by birds. For grades K-2.

Glaser, L. 1997. *Beautiful Bats*. The Millbrook Press, Brookfield, CT, 32 pp. The heartwarming story of a day in the life of a little brown bat is told with cheerful illustrations and a special section on bat facts for young readers. For grades K-2.

Greenaway, F. and J. Young. 1991. *Amazing Bats* (Eyewitness Juniors, No 13). Alfred A. Knopf, New York, NY, 29 pp. The authors provide an effective, snapshot approach to bats and their unique adaptations and lifestyles. Photographs and short sections of text discuss bat basics from nursery colonies to a midnight snack. For grades K-4.

Jennings, J. 1994. *Bats: A Creativity Book for Young Conservationists*. Bat Conservation International, Austin, TX, 30 pp. With a focus on expanding creativity, the 28 activities in this text challenge children in communication and math skills, writing, art, and more, while increasing their understanding of bats. For grades pre-K through 4.

Julivert, M. 1994. *The Fascinating World of Bats*. Barrons Juveniles, New York, NY, 31 pp. This superb nature book features vivid and scientifically accurate full-color art. Bat species are shown and described, and children learn how these flying mammals have adapted to varied climates and environments. For grades 4-7.

Lollar, A. 1992. *The Bat in My Pocket*. Capra Press, Santa Barbara, CA, 86 pp. Animal lovers of all ages will be fascinated by the details of bat behavior in this true story of the rapport between the author and an injured Mexican free-tailed bat she rescues. For grades 5 and up.

Lundberg, K. 1996. *Bats for Kids*. NorthWord Press, Minocqua, WI, 48 pp. This story joins a group of curious children as they learn about the fascinating lives of bats. Facts about natural history, hibernation, feeding, reproduction, echolocation, and more are woven into this tale of discovery. For grades 4-6.

Navarro, L. 1997. *Marcelo el Murciélago — Marcelo the Bat*. Bat Conservation International, Austin, TX, 38 pp. A bilingual story in elementary English and Spanish about a young Mexican free-tailed bat learning the ways of the world as he discovers the facts about migration. For grades K-4, and Spanish language students of all ages.

For Adults

Bat Conservation International. 2000. *Vacationer's Guide to Bat Watching*. Second Edition. Bat Conservation International, Austin, TX, 155 pp. Detailed information on more than 125 top bat-watching sites in the United States and Canada, complete with species lists and directions.

Graham, G. L. 1994. *Bats of the World: A Golden Guide*. Golden Press, New York, NY, 160 pp. A pocket-sized introduction to the world of bats and their characteristics. Includes information about distribution, taxonomy, natural history, and conservation.

Nowak, Ronald M. 1994. *Walker's Bats of the World*. The Johns Hopkins University Press, Baltimore, MD, 287 pp. The most comprehensive world bat guide available, with well-organized information on taxonomy, distribution, natural history, and physiology.

Schmidly, D. J. 1991. *The Bats of Texas*. Texas A&M University Press, College Station, TX, 188 pp. A detailed introduction to Texas bats, species accounts, and an illustrated key.

Tuttle, M. D. 1997. *America's Neighborhood Bats*. Revised Edition. University of Texas Press, Austin, TX, 98 pp. An excellent layman's introduction to North American bats, covering a wide range of issues from public health and nuisance concerns to bat values and conservation needs. Common North American bats are featured with natural history information, color photographs, a key to identification, and plans for building bat houses.

Tuttle, M. D. and D. L. Hensley. 2001. *The Bat House Builder's Handbook*. Revised Edition. Bat Conservation International, Austin, TX, 34 pp. A valuable "how to" manual on the design, installation, monitoring, and conservation impact of artificial bat roosts. Includes several easy-to-build plans and up-to-date research results on artificial roosting preferences of common North American bats.

Wilson, D. E. 1997. *Bats in Question: The Smithsonian Answer Book*. Smithsonian Institution Press, Washington, D.C., 168 pp. A user-friendly format introducing the world of bats through questions and answers highlighting the most commonly asked questions about bats, myths, misconceptions, and the need for bat conservation. This is the one resource for introductory inquiries about bats.

Activity Guides for Teachers

Bat Conservation International. 1991. *Educator's Activity Book About Bats*. Bat Conservation International, Austin, TX, 63 pp. A teacher's guide with games, crafts, and other activities for ages 4-10 that explain bat anatomy and classification and dispel common myths.

Butcher, Ginger and Beth Broadhurst, 2001. *The Adventure of Echo the Bat*. National Aeronautics and Space Administration, Washington, DC. Following Echo the Bat around the varied landscapes of Arizona teaches youngsters about both bats and their habitats and satellite imaging. Interactive online components (at images.gsfc.nasa.gov) supplement the book for a complete educational package for grades K-4.

Tuttle, M. D. 1998. *Discover Bats!* Bat Conservation International, Austin, TX, 228 pp. Book and 48-minute, 4-part video. A comprehensive multimedia curriculum comprising 21 lessons teaching essential skills in math, science, social studies, reading, and writing united under the entertaining theme of bats. For grades 4-8.

Most of these publications are available from BCI online at www.batcon.org.

Contact Information

P.O. Box 162603
Austin, TX 78716
Phone: 512-327-9721
www.batcon.org

Texas Bat Coordinator
3000 S. IH-35, Suite 100
Austin, TX 78704
Phone: 512-912-7011
www.tpwd.state.tx.us

DATE DUE